Six Cans of Jam

By Debbie Croft

Yin has a big pot.

It has a lid on top.

Yin's pot can get hot.

Yin can mix lots of red jam in her big pot.

The jam zaps and pops!

Yin has six cans.

She tips the hot jam
into the cans.

Yin lets her jam set.

Yin gets tags for her jam.

The tags go on the jam cans.

Six cans of jam are in a box.

Yin zips to see Zac.

CHECKING FOR MEANING

1. What does Yin cook her jam in? *(Literal)*

2. Who enjoys eating Yin's jam? *(Literal)*

3. Why does Yin put tags on her jam? *(Inferential)*

EXTENDING VOCABULARY

mix	Look at the word *mix*. How many sounds are in the word? What are they? What does *mix* mean? What does Yin use to mix the jam in the pot?
zaps	Listen to the sounds in this word. What are other words you know that rhyme with *zaps*? What happens when the jam *zaps*? Why does it *zap*?
set	What are different meanings of this word? Which one is used in this text? Can you change the letter *e* to make new words?

MOVING BEYOND THE TEXT

1. Do you like jam? What is your favourite type of jam?

2. What ingredients are used to make jam? Talk about how jam is made.

3. Do you like cooking? What do you like to cook?

4. Talk about why some people make their own jam and others buy it at a shop or market.

SPEED SOUNDS

Xx	Yy	Zz				
Kk	Ll	Vv	Qq	Ww		
Dd	Jj	Oo	Gg	Uu		
Cc	Bb	Rr	Ee	Ff	Hh	Nn
Mm	Ss	Aa	Pp	Ii	Tt	

PRACTICE WORDS

mix

Yin

zaps

Six

box

six

zips

Yes

Zac

yum